The Singing Is My Favorite Part

poems by
Susan Elliott Brown

More books available from:

Etched Press
www.etchedpress.com

Also available in Amazon Kindle Store

First edition
Cover art by Marika Rodrigues
Interior layout by Kevin Dublin

For Joe, the person who makes me pancakes when I need them

ACKNOWLEDGMENTS

The author wishes to acknowledge the editors of the following publications in which these poems first appeared:

Best American Poetry Blog: "Dinner Party" & "Inertia"

Measure: A Review of Formal Poetry: "Department Store, 9:45 PM"

Product: "Beatitude" & "Passenger Symphony"

Reunion: The Dallas Review: "Ode to Chest Hair"

TABLE OF CONTENTS

Take Her to Sea

The therapist's office was called *Travel On,*
but the *o* looked like a compass
or a ship's wheel, directed
lines intersecting, certain
of north and south. This was to make
it look like there's life after (*fill in the blank*):
after your husband chokes on a fish
bone at dinner, after your father runs
off with a red-haired woman who's not
even that much younger than your mom.

Like you can board
a ship and say *Ahoy, life!* without
your luggage, tossed into the dark
waves—but then what
will you wear when you arrive?

Dinner Party

A woman said a lamp in the parlor
reminded her of Michelangelo's
sculpture, but he was the only sculptor
she knew by name.
Another woman agreed and mentioned
that chapel somewhere in Europe
she thought he may have painted.
He knew the pope, right? The wine
is delightful, and probably from Italy,
like Michelangelo himself.
And the colors of the wallpaper?
Truly inspired. A balding man
passed by without notice. The women
turned to architecture, one asserted
the house was surely in the Tudor
style, while another claimed her own
was Victorian, though most everyone
assumed she lived with her mother
and a cat named Leonardo. The man
carefully selected a peach from the fruit
bowl, turning it over and over in his hands.
The women assumed him an artist,
partly because of his clothing,
guessing he'd likely paint a still
life of the peach, alone on a table
with a shadow stretching out to its left;
He must have a brilliant understanding
of light and dark, probably an expert
on the Renaissance and Europe.

Eutrophication

The dock rots beneath your feet,
fish-stale water green
around its posts. Mosquitoes
land on the oily film that thickens
the surface, dotting
its topography with sparkling
holes, like dust particles glowing
in a light beam through a basement
window. Toads breed near the teeming
banks. The air smells metallic,
the way your hands smell after
you ride the carousel at the mall,
gripping the brass pole
that impales your horse.

Nolin Lake, July 2006

On taut line a lissome bluegill
rose from the water, swinging
by its mouth and throwing
lake water onto my bare stomach.
He slid my hand down
the fish's jaws and held tight, told me
it would be sharp, fins like burs
in my skin. Watery blood drained
from its open wound and onto my
fingers, perfectly round eye fixed
in place. Tilting the hook's barb
backward through the gape, I heard
the cartilaginous clicking of face
separating from itself.

Beatitude

Her hands neatly folded in her lap
like wedding napkins, not in prayer
but in discreet listening; diamond
ring loose around a bony finger,
purple veins visible through thinning
skin like a drawing under tracing
paper. Standing, long fingers
envelop one another. Reciting

the Nicene Creed, she unfastens
and examines her clip-on earrings,
showing them to me and raising
her eyebrows. Porcelain hands
receive the body of Christ
and follow with a polite declining
of the wine from the shared chalice
and a tactful sign of the cross
—*Father, Son, and Holy Spirit*—
and a re-tying of her floral scarf.
Kneeling, she smoothes her sweater;

each garment sensibly coordinated
like vestments, her fuchsia brooch fit
for a royal family supper. She points
a foot and whispers,
*You know, I bought these pink
shoes the day after Father's Day
in 1985. I remember because
it was raining and I couldn't
find a place to park at the mall.*
She stands and slides the hymnal
between us: *Sing with me.
The singing is my favorite part.*

Oyster

He was a bold man that first ate an oyster.

-Jonathan Swift, *Polite Conversation*

Nestled inside its shallow
bed, against pearlescent
inlay, like the interior
of a music box,

lies the oyster
you will eat
on the half shell.
One hand tactically

floats under the chin
to catch the runoff,
the slimy-milky
juices that escape

after you bite
into the muscle fibers
and taste the tinge
of leftover saltwater,

pulling the last clinging
bit from the iridescent
calcifications lining
its thin-walled bed

with your teeth.

Meanwhile, Back at the House

It was never about the bread;
it was more that you forgot the milk.
I'll apologize for not doing laundry,
but I'm not the only one who forgets.

It was more about the milk anyway.
Making dinner slipped my mind tonight,
but I'm not the only one who forgets.
Did either of us feed the dogs yet?

Dinner in the oven slipped my mind
and I burned the casserole on top.
Which one of us fed the dogs?
I thought you were making dessert.

I knew I'd burn the casserole, on top
of having to apologize for the laundry.
But—really—I'm not mad about dessert,
and it was never about the bread.

Stake

Roulette is your game if you want to bet
on several different angles. Video roulette, now,
is even better if you're intimidated by people at the table. *Stop
judging my strategies.* Always looking at your bets.
You'll want to bet on evens now
because the last five have been odd. Wait for the wheel to stop.

No matter how many times you tell a husband to stop
leaving extra seconds on the microwave, you can bet
he'll do it the next day too. At first it was sometimes, but now
it's every morning. Blinking numbers, bidding me to push start *now*
when the microwave is empty. I bet
myself a hundred dollars that it's totally empty. This never stops.

I once got pulled over by a sheriff for running a stop
sign in a residential area. He said, *The sign says S-T-O-P,
not S-L-O-W.* Yes, sir. I pulled away slowly. I bet
he felt important for scaring me, probably betting
I was some neighborhood delinquent: *What's this guy up to now?*
Ready to yell until he saw it was a teenage girl. Now

that changes things. When the slot machine pays out, now
we're talking. It would certainly be wiser to stop
here, cash out—bonus will come sometime; might as well be now.
Change the wager, raise the stakes, stop,
breathe. Do it—make the bet
on the max number of lines. Repeat bet.

When do you put your parents in a home? Do you bet
on them being okay for now,
assume that if dad is healthy enough to bet
on pinochle that there's no need to stop
just taking care of him yourself? Will they stop
talking to you once they know your plans? What then? What now?

We were getting the hang of this poker thing now—
five-card draw, making bets
out of my grandfather's cup of quarters: Stop;
think about if you want to raise. Now

say, *I see your quarter, and I raise you fifty cents.* Stop
bluffing. You'll never win big on a bet

like that. Console the loser: now, now;
you can bet you'll feel better soon. Stop
that crying, you hear? Stop sulking over lost bets.

Enterprise

Empty chairs line the conference
room walls, outnumbering
company employees.
Backed up against closets
never opened, upholstery patterns
from the early eighties,
tired fabric brittle and broken.
They sit under Silver Sales Awards
from 1991; heavy plaques
pull against the wood paneling.

They wait for a meeting,
a productive gathering
of minds around the lonely
table. Dull grey file
cabinets sleep on the darkened
third floor next to mildew-heavy
Christmas wreaths and a fat
stuffed Santa. The donated
microwave *dings* in the break
room and someone waits
their turn to reheat chicken
fried rice from the Chinese
place down the street.

Push pins crowd corkboards
with outdated pictures of children,
faded and long since married off;
Personnel speak to one another
in their phone voices.

Weekend Project

First prepare the surface:
sand down the skin and minimize
freckles on the nose; exfoliation
is key to an even application.
Spackle divots if necessary. Line
the perimeter with tape, being careful
not to let stray hairs or fibers
enter the painting surface.
Don't let a fear of color turn you
into beige doldrums; bold shades
can brighten an otherwise
uninviting space.

Keep in mind the surface
you're working with—a flat finish
will hide more imperfections,
whereas high-gloss will showcase
blemishes, especially if the space
receives natural light. Sampling colors
is wise—you may think you are
Classic Tan, but a trial might prove
that you are, in fact, more of a Sandy
Neutral.

Play up the shelving units
with some blush. A soft glow makes
a great place to host guests:
try Rosy Outlook to really go for it,
or Innocent Flush if you already
have a more daring tint—
like Coral Fire—on the lip
of the crown molding,
a brave choice that will pay off
with realtors and repairmen alike.

Department Store, 9:45 PM

Attention shoppers, the store is closing
soon. Please make your final selections.
Hurry to find something exposing—

this negligee might be good for posing,
taking risqué photos for his affections.
Attention shoppers, the store is closing

in ten minutes. We don't mean to be imposing.
Find a little something in the perfume section;
without a nice scent, what's the use in exposing

some extra skin? This is all supposing
he won't notice the cellulite in your midsection.
Attention shoppers, the store is closing

in five minutes. We see you still nosing
through the face creams, hoping to mask imperfections,
but these fluorescent lights are exposing

your age spots. Buy some wine and begin composing
yourself to face inevitable rejection.
We find your purchases particularly exposing;
Attention shoppers, the store is now closing.

Ode to Chest Hair

You are
for the upper torso
what whipped chocolate
icing is for a cupcake,
what bourbon is
for Kentucky.

You are supple
sometimes,
and sometimes coarse,
both soft and hard at once,
like the Brauny Man
or a wire sponge.

You are the bear-skin
rug on the cabin
floor where we lie
by the fireplace,
running my fingers
through you.

I want to graze
in your wild grass
and feed
on your warmth,
sustenance.

I want to burrow
in you, run wild
in your thicket
and get lost
somewhere between
the areola and the navel.

Sometimes you tease:
you peek, just a bit,
above the last wayward
button on a flannel
shirt, hinting at that

torso-beard, inviting
me in to have a martini
or three
in the (five o'clock) shadow
of your clavicle.

Inertia

Before it was lit, the cigarette
lay dormant in the pack. A set
of foreign lighters from our trip
abroad didn't always have a chipped
case. Colors depict a banneret

in battle, saving a small brunette;
I'm reminded of when we met:
a cigarette balanced on your lip,
      before it was lit.

Palm skin against mine, always wet
like a humidor's sick-sweet sweat
that kept your cigars fresh, unclipped.
You'd rest one between your fingertips—
like in a silent film vignette—
      before it was lit

Past Midnight

I've always loathed the necessity of sleep. Like death, it puts even the most powerful men on their backs.

-Frank Underwood in *House of Cards (U.S.)*

Belly-up,
forearms exposed to the fan-spun
air, goosebumps hoist
your hair follicles. A spider slips
past a slack lip and you swallow
him whole, not feeling his legs
swirling against the back of your throat.

Passenger Symphony

Only classical music plays this late;
cadences float past us toward
the rear window, suspended
in the recycled air. Senses liquefy
like the pumpkin left in the trunk
that we meant to carve into some
porch decoration, a tea light inside
like a broken headlamp in the October
evening. Stop for fuel before we
hit the desolation, where hotels
are smoke-soaked and you have to ring
a bell for service, where blackened pines
mark the road to home or to someplace else.

www.ingramcontent.com/pod-product-compliance
Lightning Source LLC
Chambersburg PA
CBHW051743040426
42447CB00008B/1274